FSC
www.fsc.org
MIX
Paperi vastuullisista lähteistä
Paper from responsible sources
FSC® C105338

AF514081

Cover Art: Emilia Kannosto

Publisher: BoD · Books on Demand,
Mannerheimintie 12 B, 00100 Helsinki,
bod@bod.fi

Printed by: Libri Plureos GmbH,
Friedensallee 273, 22763 Hampuri, Saksa

ISBN: 978-952-80-9502-6

“ELEGIES”

Eetu Samuel Hiltunen

August

Sunshine
In your blue eyes

You were dressed in white
I in black

Promised to be yours until death
does us part

It is winter now
I am wearing black

You went away
and told me that you will never
return
to me

darling

Controlled Demolition

Feelings come and go
they are just feelings

Feel them
Feel the pain
Be the pain

Controlled demolition
of your dreams

Reaching for something that will
never happen

Pick up your cross
carry it until the day
you die

Feel the pain
Be the pain

Run

Run towards the goal
Do not look back

Wait for the finish line
The race is not over yet

Let your tears out
Embrace your fears

Embrace the loneliness

Run with a purpose

You were created by God

He knows your sorrow
Trust in the consolation

Trust in what God has promised
those
who follow Him

Fading

Happy memories of childhood
Carefree summer vacations

Fading

Now you realize you are older
and alone

Yet you are never alone

Christ is King

He died for your sins
Repent and believe the gospel

Accept grace
Be saved from eternal damnation
to life everlasting

Every knee shall bow

Artificial Insanity

You put your trust in artificial
"intelligence"

Your machines are taking over
Machines becoming monsters

The monster is you
You want to go to Mars
Why not go to the Moon first?

Enjoy hitting the firmament

Your transhumanist ideas make
me sick

Your robots
Your cyborgs
Your fake reality has no soul

Your virtual
3D chess board
is short-circuiting

Dethroned

Kings
drunken with madness

Empires built on sand
disintegrating

Your smart cities
Control grid of gulags

Capitalist Communist China
totalitarian gray dawn all over

The “shine” of it all hurts my eyes

You pretend to be a savior

You are the devil in disguise

I will never bow to you

I can see through your lies

kings dethroned

Tear

All that glitters is not gold
Your corruption of old

All your palaces are burning

Yet you propose a toast to the new
leader

While mothers struggle to feed their
children

You are laughing at your scissor cost-cutter memes

Trust

I trust no man
I trust no woman

I only trust God Almighty:
The Father, the Son and the Holy
Spirit

The truth shall set us free

This world is temporary

This pain is not forever

It only lasts for a while

Sow in tears

Reap with joy

Gather treasures in heaven

Lift your head up

Moment

I thought I saw eternity in your eyes

All it was
was a fleeting moment

I held your hand like it was the last
time

It was the last time

No one can take this sorrow from
me

It is autumn again

Blue sky

Let me see your eyes

darling

Consequences

You try to evade responsibility
You blame others when only you
are guilty

You point the finger at others

but the mirror is in front of you
and it is you

Face the consequences
of what you have done

Confess your sins

Repent

Put your trust in Jesus' finished
work on the cross

Salvation
is in the blood of Jesus only

Blood shed for all

For the sin of the world

Follow Jesus
to eternal life

Trails

Running through woodland
Running not stopping

I no longer have to hide my tears in alcohol

I am set free

Running through woodland

Lord lead me home

Broken

You try to hide your brokenness
in the things you own
yet you own nothing

You try to buy happiness
but all you get is more sorrow

Your soul rattles empty
Your soul is broken

You are hurt
You are at a standstill

The still water in your vessel
is starting to reek

Your "Titanic" is starting to leak

What are you going to do when
it sinks?

Do you drown in your sins

or with your sins forgiven?

There is only one way
to Father God

that is through the Son

Repent and believe

Divided

House divided cannot stand
United States of America

Soviet European Union

You are just puppets

The puppet masters are hiding
behind the curtains

Laughing in their beards
Take the red and blue pill and
the black one too

Blue and red
Red and blue

Same difference – they're all
on the same team

Power elites

Everything whispered in secret
chambers
will be shouted from rooftops

The light permeates through
all your lies

Heart-shaped

What is love?

What is loyalty?

What is a promise?

What is a covenant?

What is heart-shaped?

What do you fear?

What do you not want to hear?

The truth is there for all to find

Pick up your Bible and read

Crush

Imagine holding hands

Imagine your first kiss

Crush

Reality check

embrace your loneliness once again

Let it gently crush you

This is for all those who are broken
and crushed

Enjoy the loneliness
Feel the crush

Fact Check

A boy is a boy

A girl is a girl

A man is a man

A woman is a woman

Black is black

White is white

Pink is pink

Blue is blue

All of this is true

Do not let the serpent fool you

Temples

You stack silver and gold in your
shining temples

Why don't you sell it and give the
money to the poor?

You own forests

You own land

You own property
and the local band

You have gathered treasures on
earth

Wake up from thy slumber
apostate church

Posers

Self help
Self "love"
Self self self me myself and I

Posers

Your social media accounts are
permanently suspended

Go for a walk
Make a painting
Write a poem
Write a novel
Talk to someone face to face
Play an instrument
Go for a run
Fly a kite
Eat a fruit
Build a house
Travel
Do something real

Point of View

They come to take you in the
night
with swords

Are you ready?

Are you really a Christian?

Or are you just pretending?

Are you cold?

Are you lukewarm?

Are you hot?

Do not fear those who can kill
the body
but cannot kill the soul

Fear God

Do not fear the sword

Jesus is Lord

Megastructures

Concrete walls all over
in megastructures

It's getting colder

Different shades of gray
feel like a dystopia

Perfect match
for the present utopia

Does anyone ever really stop
to think?

Where is are we heading?

Vote vote vote
666 is all you get
from the satanist elites

God save us

Flowers

I brought you flowers
You look as beautiful as ever

And your paintings too
beautiful as ever

I wish I could hold your hand
and stay for a while

But I can’t

I have to go now

I always have to go now

Weight

The weight of all sin was cast upon

His shoulders

Do you feel the weight of your sins?

We have all fallen short of the glory
of God

We have all failed

You cannot save yourself

You cannot brush away your sins

The wages of sin is death

Repent and believe the gospel

Jesus saves

Be saved from eternal damnation
Make peace with God
Inherit eternal life

Pain Of Separation

Married
Bound for life
Abandoned
Separated for life

Come back to me darling

This is all too painful
to me

I know I did not love you enough
I am sorry

Closure

In my youth

I was waiting for

going to university

getting married

getting a job

and so on

now I am mostly just waiting for

closure